this little authoritarian

- a _mildly_ authoritative guide -

text and illustrations
by
Quentin Johnston

Dedicated to all those who dare to struggle
against their inner tyrant.

this little authoritarian - a mildly authoritative guide. Copyright © 2020 by Quentin Johnston

All rights reserved. No part of this book or elements thereof may be reproduced or utilized in any form or by any means, digitally, electronically, mechanically or otherwise without express permission of the author or the author's proxy, except for reprints in the context of literary or artistic review/discussion. Any representation of specific individuals, human or other, living or deceased, is purely coincidental, even if disturbingly accurate. This book is for educational purposes in the broadest sense of that term and any satire or sarcasm within is, in all likelihood, intentional.

Printing/Distribution: IngramSpark
First Edition: Paperback 2020
ISBN: 978-1-7357182-2-4

FOREWORD

Blah blah blah.

In all seriousness, there's not much else to say.
This book is *self-explanatory* or
maybe it's *self-exploratory*.
It's really up to *you*.

Oh, and while it by no means could be
ever considered comprehensive,
it is meant to be inclusive.

You're welcome.

Authority is much like
a delicious pie.*

* food for thought

this little authoritarian

this little authoritarian
is prone to seeking power...

..it's an inclination to domination.

this little authoritarian
believes traditions are
just rules etched in stone...

..paving the way
with good intentions.

this little authoritarian prefers a clean slate...

..for *new* and <u>approved</u> rules.

this little authoritarian believes in a god...

..and so will you, be damned!

this little authoritarian doesn't believe in a supreme authority...

..well, just not a god.

this little authoritarian thinks intelligence conveys a right to dictate the actions of others...

..it's **SIDS** - Smarts Induced Dictator Syndrome.

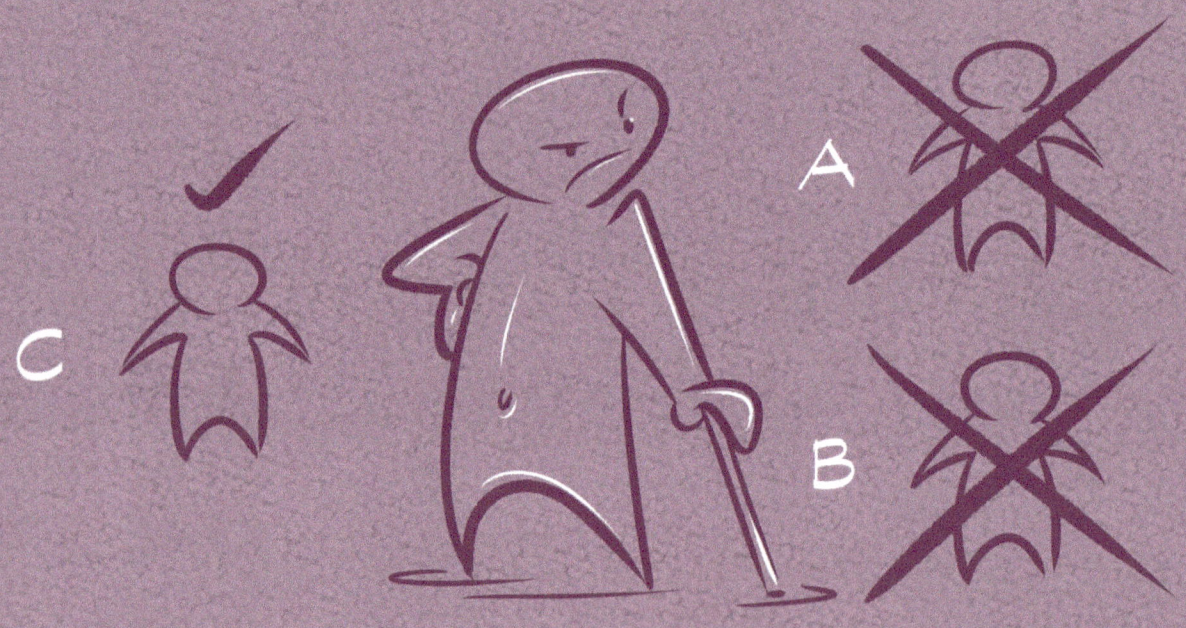

this little authoritarian
detests prejudice...

..except when it's *judiciously* applied.

this little authoritarian
loves science...

..<u>when</u> it proves its point.

this little authoritarian
demands total acceptance...

..otherwise it doesn't
take it all too well.

this little authoritarian
prefers values over facts...

..even when reality disagrees.

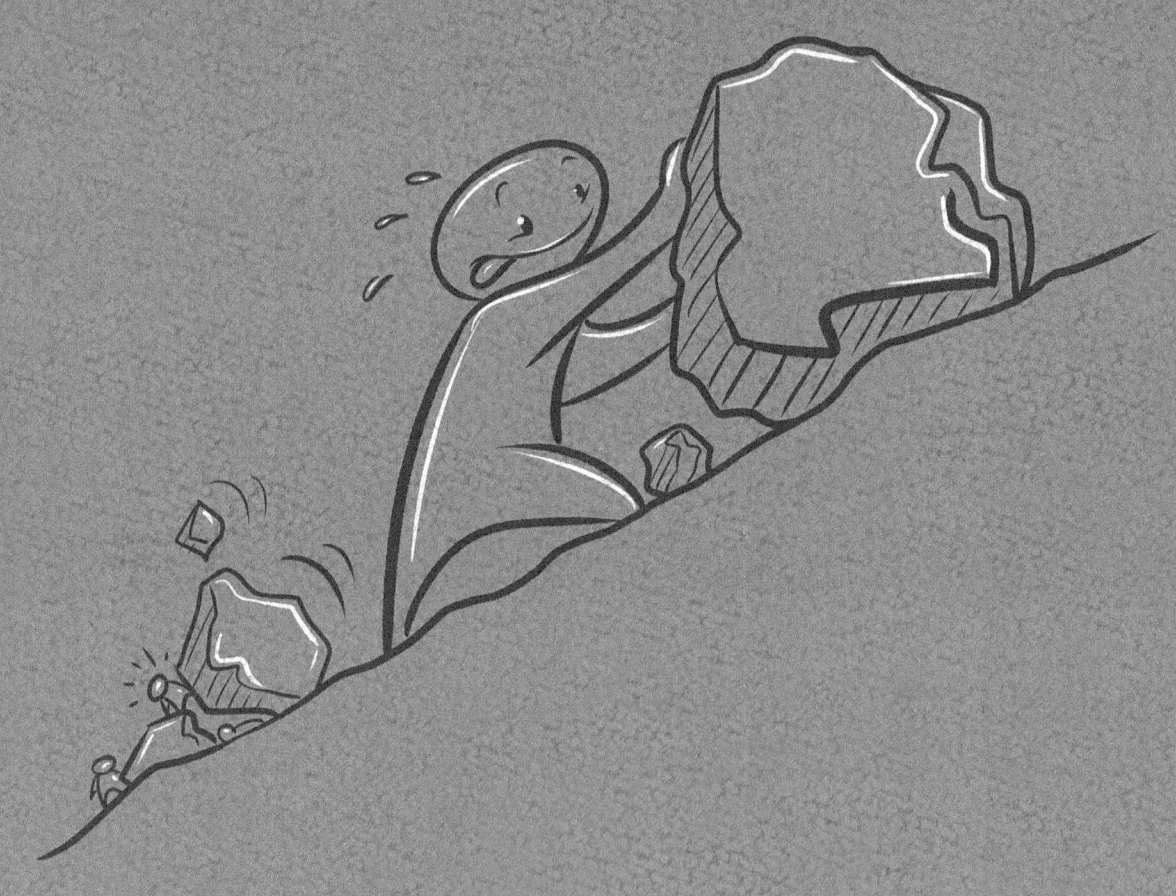

this little authoritarian
is all for tolerance...

..when it's got room for it.

this little authoritarian enjoys a healthy discussion...

..you agree, right? Right! RIGHT!

this little authoritarian
loves to guilt and shame
others for things they've done,
or even things they couldn't have ...

..but should've or shouldn't have, oh, whatever...GUILTY!

this little authoritarian
takes offense...

..whether you're giving it or not.

this little authoritarian is blessed with virtue...

..a.k.a. the curse of purity.

this little authoritarian
rallies for resistance...

..albeit <u>directionally</u> specific.

this little authoritarian has an appetite for linguistics...

..especially word salads.

this little authoritarian enjoys a good book burning...

..it must be the warmth of words.

this little authoritarian
loves to edit stories..

..it's an omission for the greater good.

this little authoritarian knows the answer is right..

..when it is all that is left.

this little authoritarian
loves democracy...

..when it's in the majority.

this little authoritarian enjoys being in the minority...

..when it rises to the throne.

this little authoritarian
thinks education is critical...

..when it's inform to conform.

this little authoritarian professes to champion the underdog...

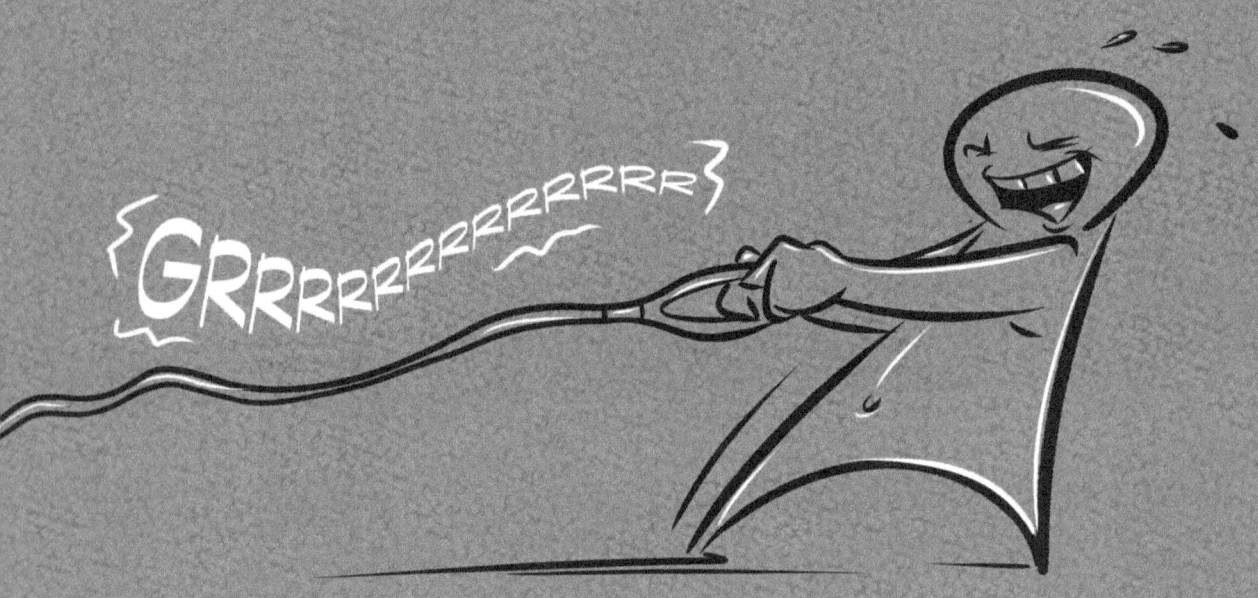

..but it's more likely the hound from hell.

this little authoritarian always has the perfect solution...

..for <u>dis</u>solving problems, and other such "nuisances".

this little authoritarian can afford to act irrationally...

..because it can <u>always</u> find a good reason.

this little authoritarian only wants a little power over others...

..but that wouldn't be you...

..would it, now?

So, authority is much like
a delicious pie.

There's simply never enough.

It's also very bloating.

www.ingramcontent.com/pod-product-compliance
Lightning Source LLC
Chambersburg PA
CBHW051120110526
44589CB00026B/2987